The Wild Banshee

– Poems for the Unruly

*To Hilary
(the lucky one!)
with friendship
+ good wishes

Bob Sheed
15/04/2014*

Bob Sheed

Copyright © Bob Sheed 2014

The right of Bob Sheed to be identified as the author of this work has been asserted by him in accordance with the Copyright, Designs and Patents Act 1988.

All rights reserved. No part of this publication may be reproduced, stored in or introduced into a retrieval system, or transmitted in any form, or by any means (electronic, mechanical, photocopying, recording or otherwise) without the prior written permission of the author. Any person who does any unauthorized act in relation to this publication may be liable to criminal prosecution and civil claims for damages.

This book is sold subject to the condition that it shall not, by way of trade or otherwise, be lent, re-sold or hired out, or otherwise circulated without the author's prior consent in any form of binding or cover other than that in which it is published and without a similar condition including this condition being imposed on the subsequent purchaser.

ISBN 9781496137180

Set in Palatino Linotype 10/12pt

Foreword

In writing this Foreword, a task I'm delighted to undertake, I have a distinct advantage over many of you who have just opened this book. I have heard Bob Sheed read many of these pieces out loud. I say 'read' but that is a wholly inadequate verb. I have heard, and seen, Bob Sheed *perform* many of these poems.

And believe me, Bob Sheed is a performer. With a repertoire of accents and even the occasional prop he can bring his work to life. With a style and wit redolent of music hall he becomes in a moment the hapless customer of a talkative barber, or a down at heel and wronged street musician. You'll meet both those characters, and many more, in these pages.

Do not however feel cheated. You're about to read poems that are more than capable of standing on their own, on the page, and they will entertain, amuse and engage you. The performance is a bonus, but the printed versions are a more than ample reward. That's because they are poems first and foremost.

This is poetry rooted in the narrative tradition and flourishing with rhythm and rhyme. There is comedy in these couplets but there is style in these stanzas. The great loops of expectancy that carry you from the end of one verse to the start of another, as the story sweeps you along, are the work of a skilled writer.

Bob once introduced me, as compere, when I was about to read some of my own work by saying 'What can I tell you about Pete Goodrum……. that isn't already known to the local constabulary?' (You see, I told you he was witty! Thanks Bob!). What can I tell you about Bob Sheed that isn't already known to you as a reader of poetry? I can tell you that he draws on tradition but is ceaselessly innovative. I can tell you that he is naturally comedic but can sting you with a line to melt your heart. I can tell you, as I already have, that he is a skilled writer, but that he is more than that; he is a born communicator. A poet.

'The Wild Bunch' is but a glimpse in to the world of Bob Sheed. Take that first look, because it's a world you'll love.

Pete Goodrum – Writer and Broadcaster
Norwich, January 2014.

Introduction

In April 2010 I wrote my first poem. I won't tell you how old I was. Let's just say I'd had years enough to write poetry on an epic scale, but hadn't. Not being allowed to study any form of English literature at school hadn't helped. My grammar school head didn't believe boys were mature enough for literature.

Eventually, I completed an MA in Writing at Sheffield Hallam University, finishing up with a collection of short stories, described by one of the external assessors as 'sound but so diverse they are probably unpublishable as a collection'.

Freeing my hand from the Vice-Chancellor's grip and clasping my diploma, I immediately enrolled on a WEA creative writing class. I needed a reason to keep writing. The first task we were given was to write a poem. My heart sank. I'd never written a poem before and had hardly read any either. The tutor put us into pairs and I was teamed up with an Iranian poet. We were asked to talk about a piece of card we had just been given. What did this blank, blue A5 sheet mean to us? Any hope of sharing my alarm with my companion was quickly dashed.

'It reminds me of the colour of the sky when I was a child, walking home from the mosque after Friday prayers, holding my dad's hand,' he said confidently. It was a delightful image that left me acutely embarrassed. I blushed at the thought that my own father had died without my ever having shared such an intimacy with him.

We broke for coffee and began scribbling. Some of the students did, anyway. I wasn't one of them. Then something clicked. Didn't the blue rectangle look a bit like a swimming pool viewed from above? Of course! My dad taught me to swim at Kingsbury Lido in north London! And he had done this by putting his hand under my chin. I picked up my pen and wrote:

'He taught me how to swim, me dad.'

Another fifteen lines followed, all in a Yorkshire way of speaking, despite neither my father nor I coming from Yorkshire. Perhaps it was being at a class in Sheffield that caused me to write in that way. It took me no more than ten minutes to finish and I've never changed a word. It appears in this collection as 'Thoughts on a Blue Rectangle.' I drove home thinking, if writing poetry's as easy as this, I'll be a poet, thank you very much. However, in the way of these things, I've never again managed to write a poem so easily.

Each of the poems in this collection has an origin that deserves a mention, but it would be tedious for us all if I went into every one. I've stuck them in only where they seem particularly interesting or useful.

Where I think a poem benefits from being read with a particular accent, I have indicated it. Speaking of which, do try to read these poems aloud. They were written to be performed.

Finally, back to those words of the MA external examiner; if my short stories were so diverse as to be unpublishable as a collection, I hope that diversity of metre, rhyme and subject in this unruly collection of poems will be no barrier to your enjoyment.

Bob Sheed 2014
Bobsheed@yahoo.co.uk

For Patricia

Contents

For the Good of her Health	01
The Ballad of the Lovesick Barber	03
Before and After	06
The Choice	07
Stardust	08
Don't Speak to Me of the Mild Coney	10
Mosaic	13
The White Elephant	14
Thoughts on a Blue Rectangle	16
Paula's Mother Arrives for Christmas	17
A Victim of Fashion	19
On Having Your Last Novel Rejected	21
The Girl with the Florin	22
Migrants	27
Barrington Bear	29
Tintin's Barber	31
The Essential Camel	33
Wasted Wishes	34
The Well-wisher	36
A New Situation	37
A Use for Anthracite	39
Gerbilacious!	42
The Hold-up	43
God's New Idea	46
The New Cleaner	49

Out with the Fairies	53
Hurricane Warning	57
Ashford-in-the-Water	59
The Night Bus	63
The Gift-Horse	66
Goldilocks	69
The Moon Shadow	73
Dreaming	74
Gender Balance	76

Littleport
The Lone Shark	78
There Lives an Old Dame	80
The Last Panda in Littleport	82
Braving the Maelstrom	84
Lizzie's Boots	86

Inspired by 'The Red Wheelbarrow' by William Carlos Williams, coupled with a rather grotesque event in a village I once lived in.

For the Good of her Health

Billy wheels his mother
in a barrow by the sea.
He brought her here from Scunthorpe
back in 1993.

Her doctor said a change of air
would benefit her chest.
A gentle walk along the beach
an ice-cream and some rest

would have her back to health quite soon,
and sound of breath again,
though anyone who's spent some time
in Cleethorpes in the rain

will tell you that recovery
is very far from sure.
For anyone who's rheumatoid,
or looking for a cure

for respiratory ailments,
coughs wheeziness and sneezes,
is bound to take a downward turn
in Cleethorpe's damp sea breezes.

Still, Billy wheels his mother
in a barrow by the sea.
He says she loves the ozone,
but she looks quite dead to me.

I once got into a conversation with a barber about his new Congolese girlfriend. I'd shared a flat at one time with a Congolese friend, so I was able to chip in a bit during the conversation, with snippets of knowledge. The more interest I showed, the more enthusiastic the barber became and the more enthusiastic he became, the more hair he cut off. I still go to see him when I'm in the area, but luckily the woman has dumped him.

The Ballad of the Lovesick Barber

In the dry heat of the barber's seat
a tale of love is told
as the scissors snip the barber slips
a comb from within the folds

of an apron grey that has seen the Day
of Judgement come and pass
while he walks the walk he's full of talk
of his new-found Congo lass

and from my head I see with dread
my lovely curls are cut
I long to say 'Your scissors stay!'
and 'Hold you hard there!' but

my fevered brain can see quite plain
-ly that the deed is done
a pile of hair beside the chair
the time to quit and run

has long gone by as now I try
to save my eyebrows lest
the clipper's blades I feel afraid
will cut them short at best

or shave them off my friends will scoff
hairless of scalp and face
my ear-lobe hair's no longer there
the clippers leave no trace

of whiskers grey I'll rue the day
I saw the barber's pole
and took my chance without a glance
at the picture on the wall

of a dark young girl with eyes like pearls
of deepest blackest jet
with coat I part he's keen to start
but his love is keener yet

of her slender legs like clothing pegs
that open to his will

his mind has gone to dwell upon
her lovely form until

he's talked all day and cut away
I wish he'd take a rest
her skin so pure I must endure
descriptions of her breasts

the Congolese have specialties
there's things he has to do
he's never done for pay or fun
an English girl to woo

he doesn't baulk though they cannot talk
a language they don't share
he's in her clutch she guides his touch
from here to there and THERE!

in time he sees up to his knees
in clippings he is stood
and a client fair he's shorn of hair
a lot more than he should

the chair swings round and fifteen pounds
I have to pay for that
 'That's great,' I say, 'I'm on my way
to buy myself a hat!'

Before and After (Yorkshire accent)

If I tell yer I used to clip poodles,
will yer ask me, 'Then what did yer do?'
Or will yer say, 'How did yer manage?
'You're clueless wi' animals, you!'

If I let on four times I've been married,
will yer jump up to be number five?
Or will yer declare, wi' yer 'ands in the air,
'You're the worst womaniser alive?'

If I weep at the death of dear Tiddles,
will yer want to know where she's interred?
Or will yer say, 'Don't worry Robert.
'She 'ad a good life so I've 'eard.'

The Choice

I never stroll around the smoke-cloaked town.
I'd rather swim with sharks in winter seas;
and if my fate says one day I will drown,
let it not be in fumes by slow degrees;

but sharply on a giant fish's tooth,
while being dragged towards a dark seabed
as images of life in age and youth
roll by like newsreel pictures in my head.

I cannot know which way the scythe will swing
to gather in the Reaper's ripened crop;
to bare my breast and welcome Death's sweet sting
or grab the hands and urge the clock to stop?

It seems that danger lurks what e'er the route
I think it's better not to venture out.

Stardust

Wesley drives a dustcart 'cross
the constellated sky,
collecting all the debris left
when starships say goodbye

to sectors of the cosmos they
may never see again
and leave a sea of high-tech rubbish
floating in their train.

He'll be the first to tell you that
it's not the greatest job,
though better than ten years in jail
for the bank he tried to rob.

He swapped the ten for two in space
with a promise of release,
if the dangerous work didn't kill him first
or an asteroid put a crease

in the back of his head where his brains once led
a life within the dome.
But in the meanwhile Betelgeuse is
where he has to roam.

And if there's time with Sirius,
the Dog Star he will play,
while collecting all the debris left
when starships go their way

Don't Speak to Me of the Mild Coney

Don't fall for the wiles of leporiphiles
who, on their mothers' graves, will swear
their witness, draped in wreaths of smiles
to blameless coney and innocent hare.

A violent creature is the rabbit:
the visceral horror of its teeth;
sundering flesh, its gruesome habit,
stripping it down to the bone beneath.

The vicious Chinchilla,
that loathsome killer,
a spiller
of innards and guts and gore.
The Giant Dutch,
escaped from its hutch,
is much
like that and even more

The Blanc de Buscat
can slaughter a rat.
The Dwarf Netherlander
can take on a gander,
or goose on the loose,
no matter its gender.

The lanky-eared Lop
is unlikely to stop
till it's ate your intestines.
Don't think to invest in
shouts of 'Blue murder!',
appeals to relent.
It's not in its nature,
this bloodthirsty creature,
to think about restin'
till fervour is spent

I swear that I once saw-a
wild-eyed Angora
that held down and tore-a
macaque limb from limb;
a fierce Himalayan
that stalked and then slay an
icy-clad yeti and feasted on him

To Kill a Bunny – Join the Fray!
While they sleep or while they play
By the Tyne or by the Tay
Cull, cull and cull again, I say.
By ridding of this scourge we may
leporiphobic dreads allay.
For this beast ten pounds I'll pay
to any who'll agree to slay

whichever specimen comes their way
and count an evening or a day
well spent, if at the end to lay
a hundred or a thousand, nay!
a million hares and rabbits grey,
or brown,
dead, upon the butcher's tray.
Come join us comrades! Don't delay!
With skinning knives their pelts we'll flay.
Cross meadows green, their blood we'll spray.
No mind the damning by the fey
who'll plead with us in great dismay
to sheathe our knives, our blades to stay.
Their arguments will not hold sway.
No quarter will our hordes display
This order we will all obey:
To slaughter now! Hooray! Hooray!

Mosaic

The man who gave birth to mosaic,
in a time we would now call archaic,
was a rather cross mason who smashed up the work
of a talented rival, a white-turbaned Turk,
who'd inlaid some marble with colourful hues:
a swirling of purples and yellows and blues.
But before the foul mason, so jealous at heart,
could whisk all the rubble away in a cart,
the Turk swept the pieces up with a brush
and returned to his studio where, without rush,
he stuck all the chippings together with spit
from a camel and wax from a candle he'd lit
for the purpose of blending a mortar-like glue,
to re-form the artwork and make it anew
in a pattern that looked like he'd meant it that way.
And that's what we call a mosaic today.

The White Elephant (Norfolk accent)

The pachyderm hev caught a germ
'at's turned his colour white.
The pallid skin hev rendered him
too sensitive to light.

The big top now they must allow
in total dark to stay
for fear the circus elephant
'll flinch and run away

'll flinch and run away, me lads
'll ill flinch and run away
to hide his plight in deepest night
and shun the light o' day

In badger friends' nocturnal dens
he'd seek to squeeze 'is frame.
An elephantine escapee,
he'd hev to change 'is name

His keeper Jack 'ould feel the lack
of income and applause;
unless to poke fierce lions
and tremble at their roars

or hev the apes perform their japes
and serve up tea to him.
No match is he for chimpanzee,
in fact he's rather dim.

So suffer not his keeper's lot
in fortune to decline.
Turn down the light for Jumbo White
in darkness now to shine.

Thoughts on a Blue Rectangle (Yorkshire accent)

He taught me how to swim, me dad,
his hand beneath me chin, 'there lad!'
he said, 'no need to fret,
t'water's warm and not too wet'.
So off I splashed in hope and fear,
knowing that me dad was near
did nought to calm me thrashing legs
that open'd and shut like clothing pegs
and when I saw him on the side
'you've left me on me own!' I cried.
'Keep going, son!' he shouted then,
'you're doing fine' and sometimes when
I think about that glorious day
my dearest memory is the way
his hand was surer than a crutch –
the only time I felt his touch

Paula's Mother Arrives for Christmas

Paula's mum drives a 12 year old Clio
like a bat out of hell? No, just Reading
spins her wheels like the great Juan Fangio
for the heights of Edale she is heading

On black ice and snow she has travelled her share
in fifty-odd years of mad driving
cutting up lorries not turning a hair
in time for the feast she is striving

To get to her daughter who's shaking with fear
that her mother will skid off the road
but the giddy old kipper's just slipping a gear
up the hill to the family abode

My God is that her doing forty at least
up the lane that road-gritters still shun?
so steep and so pitted it hasn't been policed
since the end of 2001

One headlight is blazing, the other is dead
her wipers are criss-crossed for luck
and into the grill very clearly the head
of a low-flying mallard is stuck

At the end of the drive she goes into a spin
and reverses straight up to the house
where Paula her daughter is clutching a gin
and retrieving her heart from her mouth

A Victim of Fashion

'It isn't the fashion,' old Lucifer said,
'to believe in the Devil these days.'
He let out a sigh and looked ready to shed
a tear for the passing of ways.

Now Death, who'd been stirring his coffee meanwhile,
said, 'Take my advice on this score.
I show myself daily, I've made that my style,
so all the world holds me in awe.

'But when were you last out of Hell? Tell me that!
I've not seen your face on the news.
You've got to get out more, I'm telling you flat.
You really don't have an excuse.

'There are plenty of times, you've got to concede,
when the credit is your due alone:
a mining disaster; some terrible deed;
a gunman whose senses have flown.

'But what do folk do? They go to the church
and send all their prayers up to God.
They say, "It's His will," leaving you in the lurch,'
and here Death gave the Devil a prod

with the pitchfork his friend had leaned next to his chair,
which made the Old Antichrist jump.
'You can do it old chum, you've still got the flair,'
and he slapped Baalzebub on the hump.

But the Angel who fell could not be bucked up,
though for Heaven he'd once made a bid.
He wound in his tail and put down his cup.
Then he went to the toilets and hid

his face in his hooves; he wept floods of tears
and against the injustice, he railed.
'I've done a good job, all down the years.
I'm a victim of fashion!' he wailed.

In Sympathy On Having Your Last Novel Rejected

My heart bleeds for you Author dear
You hang your head in shame
Your agent's blighted your career –
Her reasons oh so lame!

She says your work's not up to scratch
Your hero is a clot
The style of prose is not a patch
On last time and the plot

She says you've gone and borrowed
From one that Archer stole
And even then the novel bombed
I'd say that on the whole

You're better off without the bitch
There's always Amazon
Your fortunes they may not enrich –
Your talent's clearly gone

But friends can all write praises
And hand out stars in fives
While she can go to blazes
As your reputation thrives!

The Girl with the Florin

In the street she came up to me, pausing in front
of the hat I had placed on the ground,
and cocking her head on one side like a bird,
tapped her foot to the musical sound
that was coming from out of the box as I turned
the handle around and around.

How ragged she was: she had only one shoe,
and that with a hole in the toe.
If I'm hoping for tuppence from this little wretch
then I'm madder than ever I knew.
So I turned from her, winking at Sammy instead,
the monkey who's part of the show.

T'was the clink of a coin going into the hat
that made me look back with a start.
She was walking away from the florin she'd dropped
in the hat and was boarding a cart.
'Come back' I called after her, 'this is too much,'
for the sight of her struck at my heart.

She seemed to be turning the thought in her head,
whether to ride off or stay.
In the end it was Sammy grabbing her frock
that decided the fate of the day.

He pulled her along, it was almost as though
he could tell the part she was to play.

'What are you doing, you foolish young child?
A florin's a guinea to you.
Why give it to sops for their Guinness and mild,
while you're still in want of a shoe?
My hat's spilling over, with coinage it's piled.
No need of the florin you threw.'

In silence her eyes put me right on the spot.
She had seen just how few coins there were,
the greatest of which, a thruppenny piece,
silver metal among the copper,
brought the total to not much above two and six.
The truth she was quick to infer.

'For your poverty sir, I take share in the blame,
now that mother is no longer here,
for a debt undischarged is a stain on the soul.
My mother's good name I must clear.
The disgrace that befell you, that lost you your job,
was caused by the one I held dear.'

Fourteen years had gone by since misfortune had struck,
though I'll always remember the day,
when drunk at the reins of an old horse-drawn bus,

I had quite lost control of the dray
and run a wheel over the foot of a man
who by ill luck had stood in the way

T'was nobody's fault but my own, I declare,
so what was this young girl about?
Puzzlement clearly was writ on my face,
for without more ado she set out
to recount the events she had learnt from her ma,
in a death-bed confession, no doubt

'Fourteen years ago on a cold winter's eve,
a girl of sixteen sat in tears,
at the back of a bus, the last one that night,
homeless and wretched, she feared
that another night spent on a mattress of snow
would leave a stark corpse to be cleared

from the pavement in Wapping the following morn,
and no one to pray for her soul.
She begged the conductor for leave to remain.
In return she would give him her all.
She'd traded her body like that once before.
Her honour had nowhere to fall.

For that night at least she had somewhere to lie,
and the man did not use her for long.

*She found the next morning he'd covered her up
with a coat, and although she'd been wronged,
she was grateful he'd taken the trouble to care.
It was clear that to him it belonged*

*for the badge of the company owning the bus
was pinned to the jacket's lapel.
She recited the number again and again,
so from memory one day she could tell
of the man who had saved her from death on the street,
and the clang of the funeral bell.*

*But before she departed, her fortune to meet,
in the pocket she slipped her young hand
and felt the rough edge of a new silver coin,
though of "thief" she should not bear the brand.
She took it as payment for use of her flesh,
as would any girl in the land*

*It was many weeks later she heard of the news,
that her saviour had since lost his post.
For the florin the comp'ny must surely have missed
and upon her poor shoulders a host
of regret and self-loathing piled high in a heap
and her soul irretrievably lost.'*

'You've done well to find me,' I said with a sigh,
'for my tale's not well known in these parts.
But I'll not take the florin, it isn't my due.
listen hard and <u>my</u> story I'll start.'
But before I began she collapsed into sobs
'You're my father, I know in my heart!'

And that is what did it for me on that day.
The truth I will take to my grave.
It was Bill the conductor who, guilty as sin,
had run off in the way of a knave,
and left me to cover the wretch with <u>my</u> coat –
the life of the young girl to save.

Now there are three of us making our way
round the streets of the West End and Strand.
I turn the handle while Rosie's pure voice
sings the words of songs simple and grand.
And Sammy she's taught a useful new trick:
dipping pockets with his little hand.

Migrants

Consider neighbour, if you will,
the hairs within your own nostril
which, rooted in the dark and damp,
may wish to your moustache decamp;

to join the likeness of a rat
on upper lip and savour that
last dribble of tomato soup
that lingers on the sodden droop;

until a length of leathery tongue
licks it out from in among
the crumbs of toast and flecks of cheese;
a speck of nutmeg; basil leaves

and other remnants of repasts
whose traces, never meant to last,
live on in bushy forest deep,
memories of past meals to keep.

Compared with dwellers in the nose,
where smells are rarely of the rose,
the moustache lives the gourmet life
on cuisine left by fork and knife.

Consider neighbour, if you will,
the hairs *without* your own nostril,
and trim them not from their ambition,
but let them grow, sans inhibition

Barrington Bear

Her mum told her not to go flirting with him,
    (Millicent Havers from Kent):
that boy from the house cross the river from them,
    who'd left her dad's car with a dent
in the front of the door on the passenger side
    when a brick he'd thrown famously went
a little bit further than he'd had in mind
    and although no offence had been meant
Mum went on alarming 'bout "transpontine" folk
    and their shameful display of contempt
for everyone living this side of the bridge,
    paying mortgages rather than rent.

'You've got it all wrong you bone-headed trout,'
    shouted Millie, unleashing her tongue.
'It was ignorant dick-heads from over *this* side:
    hee-hawing arseholes who slung
insults at Barry and jeered that his mum
    had stood by the co-op and flung . . . . . . her knickers
at men for the points on their dividend cards,
    no wonder her husband had wrung
her neck, till her eyes shot like corks from her head.
    "Three cheers for Popeye!" they'd sung.
Little wonder he let fly an answering brick,
    as the spring of his anger was sprung.'

'I'm sorry, I'm sure,' said her mum, with a huff,
    'you can marry the twerp, I don't care.
But I'll not let his murdering dad through the door,
    you can have the reception elsewhere!'
'We seem to be getting ahead of ourselves,'
    said Mill, 'please allow me to share
my thoughts on the subject of marriage to one
    who so far has failed to declare
an int'rest in anything more than his dogs
    and breaking up old cars for spares.
And d'you seriously think I would marry a man
    with a handle like "Barrington Bear"?'

Tintin's Barber

I don't know why I'm going to the barber's.
I don't know why I'm heading there at all.
I know the fearful plan the barber harbours –
the fate that to my hair will soon befall.

His question 'how much off this time?' disguises
the fact that never mind what I reply,
as every customer now realises,
he only has one style, so by and by

the entire male population of the parish
comes to look like Hergé's Tintin, tuft atop.
And no matter how much hairgel you may lavish
that defiant sprig will always spring back up

An exception to this rule: my neighbour, 'Cannon';
so named because his head's a billiard ball.
He's rarely seen around without his cap on
and he doesn't fear the scissors snip at all.

So I wonder what he's doing going in there,
dodging past the CCTV's prying lens,
and slipping like a weasel to its lair there
disappears into the back room of his friend's.

For friends they must be surely I am certain.
Why else would Barber Bill lock up the door?
And to thwart my nosy gaze, draw down the curtain,
which excites my curiosity more and more.

I slip around the back in agitation.
I suspect I know what's going on within.
And sure enough I glimpse in confirmation
evil Cannon, through a window, in his sin.

He's trying on a wig of glorious texture,
with curls that bounce and shimmer, shake and shine.
A professional job has made a lifelike fixture
from a head of gorgeous hair that once was mine.

The Essential Camel

I'm looking for the bloke who stole my camel.
My journey I have only just begun.
My plans this wretched thief has sought to trammel.
I may not get to see the setting sun

on the ramparts of the fort where young Beau Gest-e
turned back a sea of murderous Berber swords,
while penning notes of love to girlfriend Esther
and teasing from his banjo, tender chords.

I could cadge a lift but hate to be beholden
to a fellow caravanner on the road.
Yet how else shall I ride the dunes so golden
and give some meaning to this woeful ode?

Oh look, a Turk, beside his mount asleep.
I'll slip its halter, then away I'll creep!

Wasted Wishes

I've never wasted time on making wishes.
I give the chicken's breastbone to the cat;
and wishing wells are best left to the fishes,
while the four-leafed clover I wear in my hat,

is actually a shamrock with delusions
that girls will want to kiss it on the spot
and make a wish in haste or in confusion
that they'll get pregnant; either that or not.

Don't cover it with candles burning brightly,
should you think of baking me a birthday cake.
My attempts to blow and wish would be unsightly.
You'd find it was a terrible mistake

to have me cover one and all with splutter.
I wouldn't wish to spoil the party frocks
of ladies or the gentlemanly schmutter,
by soaking them from collars to their socks.

I'd love to wish you well upon your journey:
bon voyage, appétit, gezunterheit;
that you'll never need to find a good attorney;
that in the end your luck will turn out right.

But I know that in the very act of wishing,
I'll condemn you to a life without a dime.
So don't say, "Wish me luck, I'm going fishing,"
'cause your net will come back empty every time.

The Well-wisher

My well-wisher pastes letters crudely torn
From newspapers and shiny magazines
The message: I should never have been born

The product of a wanton satyr's spawn
Reared by satanic harridans and fiends
My well-wisher pastes letters crudely torn

The angels at my birth stood all forlorn
And wept to view the unbecoming scene
The message: I should never have been born

To ward off evil Gabriel blew his horn
And turned on me the venom of his spleen
My well-wisher pastes letters crudely torn

Be'elzebub was there that evil dawn
And at my elbow has for ever been
The message: I should never have been born

To slay an infidel if I be sworn
My soul immortal I may yet redeem
My well-wisher pastes letters crudely torn
The message: I should never have been born

A New Situation (Yorkshire accent)

Since we're in the 'ere and now,
I'll not complain o' past infractions;
I'll not condemn yer selfish actions;
I were me and you were you
and that's the end o' it, McGrew.
Since we're in the 'ere and now.

Since we're in the 'ere and now,
I'll not remind yer of occasions
you left me wi' severe abrasions;
laughed it off as though t'were naught,
then cycled off wi'out a thought.
Since we're in the 'ere and now.

Since we're in the 'ere and now,
I'll not refer yer to the caning
I took fer you wi'out complaining.
You broke the glass and fingered me;
I learned that that's how it 'ould be.
Since we're in the 'ere and now.

Since we're in the 'ere and now,
I'll not berate yer fer yer scheming –
the dreams o' wealth you 'ad me dreaming.
Too late now to count the cost.

I'll not reveal how much I lost.
Since we're in the 'ere and now.

Since we're in the 'ere and now,
I'll not discuss the girl I married.
You stole 'er, wi' the babe she carried,
told the lad he were yer own.
I never saw 'im; now 'e's grown.
Since we're in the 'ere and now.

Since we're in the 'ere and now
in war, I'll tell yer my suspicion:
you bought yer officer's commission,
which put you at the front today
when screaming mortars came our way.
Since we're in the 'ere and now.

A Use for Anthracite

My father fashioned likenesses
of great men of his day:
Richard Nixon, Henry Kissinger,
Don Rumsfeld, and the way

he carved their features
earned the praise of every one.
For he brought out all the goodness,
and the lies that they had spun

seemed impossible to credit
from the earnest, tender eyes
they turned to their creator
who managed to disguise

the evil that oozed out of them
in truth from every pore.
But when an ex-prime minister
came knocking at the door,

my father turned a sickly grey
and staggered to a chair.
'Oh please don't ask me to do this,
I beg you, Mr Blair.

There's a limit to my talents,
a paucity of skill,
when it comes to carving men of faith
who didn't pause to spill

the blood of those he sent, to fight
a war that wasn't theirs,
with insufficient armour
and jeeps that lacked for spares.

For how I am to craft
a loving turning of those lips
that speak of God while from
the snake-split poisoned tongue there drips

a trail of false assurances,
statistics that deceive,
while the tragedy of orphans
and widows left to grieve

can't prompt you to say "sorry"
for the chaos that you caused.'
But here my dad drew breath
and in his frenzied ranting, paused.

'Still, brass is brass,' he said
and wiped the cold sweat from his brow.

'I'll not turn down good business,
since we're in the here and now.'

And scrabbling in his workbox,
chose a lump of anthracite.
'It's dark and rather grimy,
so for you should carve just right.'

Gerbilacious!

A new generation of gerbils is born!
The purple rhinoceros is blowing his horn!
Let's saddle a peacock and ride off at dawn!

With rapturous whoopings a crowd will be drawn
by the tidings we bring them this jubilant morn.
Their hearts will be lifted, their throats will be worn

hoarse by their shouting, their clothes will be torn
as they rip off their smocks, to abandonment sworn:
the sheep's in the meadow, the cow's in the corn

and all kind of mayhem, though none looks aghast.
They run helter-skelter, (who wants to be last!?)
in this race to the place where the gerbils surpassed

all expectation, they're breeding so fast
that the cage to contain them (decidedly vast)
is bursting apart, can one help but contrast

this with years of sterility (certainly passed)
when the breeders of gerbils could not have amassed
such numbers that soon they may have to be gassed?

The Hold-up

In 1871 Wild Bill Hickok, while marshal of Abilene,
Kansas, attempted to relieve the outlaw John Wesley
Hardin of his pistols. Contemporary accounts offer
different versions of the outcome. The event inspired me
to write the following piece set in the present day.

Welcome to Abilene, pardner.
Just drop your gun there by the door.
There's a new law, says Barack Obama –
you <u>can't</u> shoot folk up any more.

Does that *make* any sense to you, stranger?
What about when we next go to war?
How d'yer make kids aware of the danger
if they've never been shot at before?

We need learning about life's surprises –
being ready for fortune to turn.
Like banks in their Santa Claus' guises,
when they thought they had money to burn,

handing <u>cash</u> out to winos and junkies.
"Let 'em dream the American dream!"
They might *just* have well lent it to monkeys.
To me that's the way it'd seem.

And these health plans are plain idiotic –
helping pregnant young girls to abort.
Having babies is real patriotic.
Ain't that what, as kids, we were taught?

Well, I can't hang round yakking all day, son.
Can I get you some chips and a beer?
And I'd like it if you laid that hand gun
with the others guys' weapons round here,

in this box on the shelf by the counter,
or the sheriff'll have me for lunch!
Even though he'll eventu'lly get round ter
saying laws are put there by a bunch

of guys with the livers of chickens,
in comf'table armchairs back East,
paid an emperor's fortune for stickin'
their noses in places they're least . .

Hey buster what's that you're a-doin'?
Don't point that six-shooter at me.
I tell yer, it's easy to ruin
a friendship, say buddy let's see

if we can't talk this out nice and easy –
shake hands, though we may disagree
on the ethics of hold-ups and murder,
in this wonderful Land of the Free!

God's New Idea

"I've got something new," said Moses the Jew,
"I've chiselled it down on a rock –
a list of a few . . . things you must do
and some you must not; here's a shock:

there's no room for doubt, adultery's out,
and you'd better not covet that ox
in the neighbouring field; when He said that, I reeled.
I tried to persuade Him, I vow,

that stealing from goys is one of our joys
and surely it can't be a sin
for one who employs good Jewish boys
to steal for our kith and our kin.

And that's not the end, oh Heaven forefend
we should take the Lord God's name in vain.
So don't say 'Oh God!' but rather, 'Oh sod!'
Or His fearful revenge you'll entrain.

Now some things are clear that won't cost us dear.
I'll not bear false witness to that.
We'll do it His way, He'll not have us pray
To other gods, Baal and Anat

Your mum and your dad will really be glad
if you honour them: do as they say.
If you can't, just pretend, you know in the end
you're bound to get your own way.

And you'd better not kill, for profit or thrill,
or you'll have the old boy in a rage.
We might challenge His Will at some time but still
it's best we obey at this stage.

I'm afraid there is more, he got very sore
when I told him each Saturday night
we get into teams, everyone screams
and we kick a sheep's bladder about.

But this idea He's got that the Sabbath must not
be used for sport, driving or toil,
on our day is a blot, on His laws He is hot –
Commandments that seem set to spoil

all our innocent fun when we only get one
day off work and to play we're inclined.
'The Sabbath keep holy, play no roly-poly
and don't tell me you have just signed

with a Premiership club, for here is the nub:
My commandments you'll keep to the verse –

no images make, in your shoes you will shake.
I am wrathful, for better or worse.'

Then we had a long talk about eating pork
but he said to keep shtum about that.
He's fond of a bite of bacon, all right.
That's probably why he's so fat.

Things could have been worse. Just think what a curse
it would be if he'd told us to care
for the sick and the lame and oh what a shame
if our fish and our loaves we'd to share.

Now it's back to the wife, the trouble and strife.
She'll be bending my lug-holes tonight.
'What about women's place in His chosen race?'
She may have a point there, all right.

The New Cleaner

We've got a new cleaner: she's foreign and fat.
She brings her young daughter, who chases the cat.

"She just want to stroke 'im," the mother complains
and pulls a long face at whoever explains

that the moggy is old and best left alone.
I smile through my teeth and hope that the tone

in my voice won't provoke her to elbow that vase
or iron too roughly my lacy peignoirs.

"The 'oover is broken, kaput, busted, yes?"
Well, not till you dropped it down stairs; at a guess

that might be the reason it's making a sound
like the crashing of cars on the Devil's Fairground.

My furniture, curtains and general décor,
she tells me my neighbours would wholly deplore.

Their houses are full of the latest designs
and as for the state of my IKEA blinds,

they won't last a fortnight – how tatty they look!
I decline to point out that in fact all it took

was her daughter to swing like a chimp on the cord
and poke through the slats with a plastic toy sword

at the cat on the windowsill, jabbing his paws
and scratching the wood with his well-sharpened claws.

"Do you 'ave any wodka?" she asked yesterday.
"For cleaning the silver, there's no better way."

Is that why our bottles of vodka and gin
have been going down since the day she walked in?

I don't like to leave her alone in the flat
She says she won't smoke but I'm noticing that

when I pull out the rubbish bag lining the bin
a cascade of dog ends she thought she'd put in

have slipped down the side and now cover the floor.
I really don't think I can take any more

of this woman who, rather than easing my day,
is making my 'vita' far less than 'dolce'.

My husband says, 'Don't let it bother you, pet,'
and it's true that he's more easy going, and yet

it's rather disturbing, I can't help but see,
when he thinks I'm out of the room he feels free

to give her plump buttocks a pat or a stroke.
So tactile – it's lovely with that sort of bloke,

but surely that's going a little bit far?
And he whispers to her, she's his favourite char!

I've moaned to my friends and asked their advice.
Each one of them says that it's not very nice,

but what can you do, when you can't get the staff?
And d'you think she would look at your Fred? What a laugh!

So I'm left feeling doubly insulted and now
I think, is it worth it, having a row?

* * *

She's been here a month, and she told me today
She's entitled to sickness and holiday pay.

She wants some time off, to visit her mum
and could I look after the kid while she's gone?

It's just for a week, I surely won't mind
I ask why's she leaving her daughter behind.

She gives me a shrug, as though I should know,
and I nod 'cause my husband says, "Go with the flow!"

It's all right for him, he's going away
for a week on a job; where to, he can't say.

It's very hush-hush, a government thing.
When he gets to the airport he'll give me a ring.

He says not to worry, he's not going far.
In the meantime the cleaner's got into his car.

She's on the same flight, he could hardly refuse
to give her a lift; she's begun to abuse

our kindness I feel, what with this and the child
who's used to being allowed to run wild.

We wave as the car pulls away from the kerb:
to my lips, with an 'f', comes an old English verb.

Out with the Fairies

"It's a year to the day since we sat in the tub,
laughing and drinking champagne.
Our friends had all taken themselves to the pub,
when suddenly down came the rain.

You covered my glass with the flat of your hand,
and I did the same thing to yours.
Which one of us said, 'Let's try and stand'?
We struggled to get on all-fours.

Gripping our glasses, two hands on each one,
from all-fours we stumbled to two.
My knee caught your nose – blood started to run
I said, 'I know just what to do!'

I rushed off to get a handful of ice
from the bucket we'd left by the door.
But the darn thing had gone and although I looked twice
it just wasn't there any more."

> ° ° ° *Oh yes, Billy boy, I remember it well.*
> *Of the dangers you hadn't a clue!*
> *or you'd never have ventured alone to the dell,*
> *'midst the sorrel and borage and rue,*
> *heedlessly drawn by the summoning knell*
> *of campanulas beckoning you.*

"I hurried away in search of some dock.
I'd a notion it's useful to quell
the flow of a nosebleed, I tripped on a rock.
Into Stygian darkness I fell."

> ° ° ° *It was thus to the Kingdom of Fairies you came,*
> *I joined you 'midst nettle and sage,*
> *where the Princess of Pixies claimed you in her name.*
> *When denied, she flew into a rage*
> *for her father, the King, was not minded the same.*
> *His relent was to grant her an age*
>
> *of a year and a day to await your return,*
> *Only then to be placed in her hand*
> *would you be, Billy boy, though your plight you'd not learn*
> *from my lips, for to them speech was banned.*
> *So I strive by my thoughts your freedom to earn;*
> *to prevent your return to their land.*

"I've got no idea what I did after that
My mind was left totally blank.
All night on the decking I seem to have sat
yet I wonder my love why you shrank

from speech the next day and each day ever since,
as though you are under a spell;

serene as a princess, awaiting your prince;
as soft as a pale aquarelle.

On a breeze through the garden, you drift like a wraith,
borne along by a current of air.
That one day you will speak again, dare I have faith?
In the meanwhile, with silence forbear?"

> ° ° ° *Be wishful your prayers be not met, Billy boy,*
> *till a year and a day have expired.*
> *Only then will the fairy-folk cease their annoy*
> *and the curse upon me be retired;*
> *But should you be captured 'ere that, Billy boy,*
> *then the pyre of your doom will be fired.*

"There are times when I think that I hear in my head,
some monologue, barely a snatch;
your voice all a-tremble – an echoing dread
though there's never a word I can catch.

You show me so little. I wait for a sign,
but patience is hard to exert.
I watch as you sleep and try to divine
to our old lives how we might revert.

Yet whenever I speak of the hollow that lies
at the foot of our garden, my love,
a look of dire pleading comes into your eyes
and denies my return to the grove.

It's a year and a day since we drank that champagne.
Superstition has no hold on me,
yet a feeling persists that I must go again
to the end of the garden and see

whatever it was that rendered you dumb
and all memory swept from my head.
The depths of the mystery I'm ready to plumb,
and tonight I will not be gainsaid!"

That was when I jumped up and grabbed hold of the spade
that someone had left by the fence.
I gave him a whack on the head that soon laid
him out and removed every sense.

Quietly sleeping he lay until dawn,
till the morning sun broke on his face.
And a new day began by the clock of the faun.
The Princess had just lost the race.

The hurricane that struck central and southern Britain on the 28th October 2013 had been predicted, but it arrived a few hours late. TV crews who had been despatched to coastal areas found themselves standing on beaches against a background of waves which, although a bit on the vigorous side, didn't look likely to bring about the devastation newsroom bosses were hoping for. Desperate for something to say, they told us repeatedly that things were really bad on the Isle of Wight

Hurricane Warning

A hurricane will hit the coast tonight
Reporters are despatched to sea-smashed shores
Strong winds are battering the Isle of Wight

The newsroom anchor hopes the forecast's right
an anticlimax, something he deplores
A hurricane will hit the coast tonight

And yet clear skies still show the moon's calm light
as panic spreads across the studio floors
Strong winds are battering the Isle of Wight

When will the promised storm come into sight?
to shatter glass, lift roofs and break down doors?
A hurricane will hit the coast tonight

From Brighton beach he's desperate to excite
his viewers with real news, but clasps at straws
Strong winds are battering the Isle of Wight

No-one's been sent to view the Island's plight
It counts for nothing once the storm withdraws
A hurricane will hit the coast tonight
Strong winds are battering the Isle of Wight

Ashford-in-the-Water

At Ashford-in-the-Water,
in the Peaks of Derbyshire,
you'll marvel at its beauty,
at any time of year.
And in this place some wondrous things
and people you will see,
from city types to landed lords
and sturdy peasantry.

At Ashford-in-the-Water,
all the dog-poo bins are green,
while those in every other place are red;
you will have seen
how careless folk mistake them
for a post-box in their haste
to catch the last collection,
drop their letters in the waste

of curly-coated poodles,
cocker spaniels and pekes,
but in Ashford-in-the-Water
no-one has to wait for weeks
for Canine Ordure Operatives
to sort the mail from turds.
I'd love to sing their praises,
but I just can't find the words.

At Ashford-in-the-Water,
on the famous Sheepdip Bridge,
stands a woman who reminds me
of Dame Edna Everage.
In gaudy frock and glasses,
with a gladdie in her hair,
she flings her arms and scatters bread
to ducks, so that the air,

at first so calm, is quickly filled
with ducks' excited quacks,
that set the dogs to barking
and one owner to attack
his neighbour, shouting,
'Why the *hell* can't you control
your dog, you selfish pig?'
and picking up a water bowl,

tips a mixture of foul liquid,
dog dribble and some spit
on the owner of a pug who's shouting,
'Rufus, damn you, sit!'
But the dog, ignoring orders,
has some ideas of his own
and sinks his teeth through sock and flesh
down to the ankle bone
of an innocent old lady

who wouldn't hurt a flea.
As witness to injustice,
she tries involving me.
But I'll not be distracted
from my duty to my art.
I hurry off in diligence,
at once to make a start

upon the epic poem
which I lay before you here,
making light of those misfortunes
that cost other people dear.
'All art is based on suffering':
I hold this to be true.
But if I get to make a choice,
I'll see the pain's on you.

At Ashford-in-the-Water,
the guide-book plays a prank
when it sends you through an iron gate
that closes with a clank
behind you, barring exit from a field
in which some cows
are displaying body language
that says more than mere 'How now?s'

At Ashford-in-the-Water
there are first-aid volunteers
who are trained to deal with tourists
who have hoof prints on their rears.
They can patch up cuts and scratches
with a bandage and some lint,
and sort out trample injuries
with sutures and a splint.

Of the flavour of this village
I have given you a whiff,
Enough, I hope, to bring you here
one sunny day and if
the exuberance of bovines
overwhelms you by and by,
at Ashford-in-the-Water,
there's no prettier place to lie.

The Night Bus

She's sitting on an N13
Clapham Common Bus.
It hasn't moved for ages
but she's loath to make a fuss.
There's bound to be a reason
for the omnibus's torpor.
Though she's paid the fare, with cash to spare,
in courage she's a pauper.

She looks around in hope of finding
that she's not alone.
Perhaps a fellow-passenger
could ask what's going on.
Maybe a bolder person from
her awkwardness will shrive her,
who'll dare defy the notice that says
'Don't distract the driver.'

But the vehicle's as empty
as a hanging judge's heart –
the sort of emptiness that
makes you wonder if Descartes
himself might start to doubt
his shibboleth, oft quoted:
'I think, therefore I am',
in his philosophy demoted,

for like the tree that crashes down
unheard within the wood,
if there's nobody around
to see us on a bus, we could
begin to feel we don't exist –
perhaps we are just dreaming,
or in another universe,
where Scotty does his beaming.

She wants to taker herself in hand,
to concentrate her mind.
'You're a typical example
of rational womankind!'
Though clearly overstating things,
that makes her feel much better.
She wonders now why she
has let this episode upset her.

She leaves her seat and boldly walks
up to the driver's cab,
when suddenly the vehicle starts,
so fast she has to grab
the handle of the driver's door.
The fear she thought she'd banished
returns at once the moment
that she sees the driver's vanished.

The mystery of the missing night bus,
number N13
has flummoxed transport bosses
from Hayes to Golders Green.
No driver was on shift that night,
so how the bus got going
and left no trace on camera,
there really is no knowing.

The Gift-Horse

I looked the gift-horse in the mouth.
It whinnied, 'Please refrain!
These dentures don't belong to me.
By whose legerdemain,
they got into my oral tract,
I've yet to ascertain.

They're surely meant for ass or mule;
for donkey or giraffe.
I'd be *very* pleased if you'd put in
a word on my behalf
to the jocund folk in charge round here
who've done this for a laugh.'

I suggested to the haughty nag,
if he didn't like the teeth,
why couldn't he just spit them out?
'Neigh, neigh! T'would be beneath
an Arab thoroughbred,' he cried.
'It's quite beyond belief.

Do *I* look like a camel, sir,
who'd spit as soon as wink?
My sire I'll not dishonour sir,
so have another think.

Though you lead me to the water, sir,
you'll never make me drink.'

I told the equine not to get
his withers in a twist.
'You're not a real horse, anyway,'
I ventured to insist.
'You're nothing but a proverb, mate.
You really don't exist.'

That should have been the end of it,
high time for me to go,
and off I would have shuffled,
but then down upon my toe
came a hoof as real as any full-blood
thoroughbred could show.

'You brute!' I cried, I clutched my foot
and staggered round and round.
'You've wandered from a knacker's yard
for clichés, I'll be bound!'
The gift-horse shook his head
and then he gently pawed the ground.

'A proverb's not a cliché, sir –
please show me some respect,
for truths that come from horses' mouths
you never should neglect.
Upon these words of wisdom
I suggest you might reflect:

Don't question what you're given, sir.
Receive it with good grace.
Generosity may not enfold
fine taste in its embrace,
yet still say "Thank you, friend!"
and show it plainly on your face.'

Before I could regain my wits,
the horse began to choke
me with his martingale,
I gave a soundless croak,
and wrestling with a twisted sheet,
at this point I awoke.

Bearsville (pop 702) is a hamlet in Ulster County, New York State. It gets its name from a German peddler and storekeeper Christian Baehr, who settled there in 1839 – nothing to do with bears, then; except that, on July 13th 2012, a woman reported a family of bears repeatedly breaking into her kitchen and ransacking her house.

Goldilocks and the Three Bears

There's a diner on the interstate,
run by a blue-eyed blonde
who's known to all as Goldilocks.
Her fame extends beyond

the tresses of her yellow hair
that give the girl her name.
Her ham and eggs with honey are,
by general acclaim,

the best you'll find in New York State.
for Bearsville is the place
she lost her heart to honeyed ham
and thought it no disgrace

getting drunk on honey wine
and climbing in the trees;

competing recklessly with bears;
stealing honey from the bees.

The bears tried to surround her –
they were of a single mind.
If she didn't have a bear in front
she had a bear behind.

She'd not give up the honey,
though they broke into her home,
smashed up all the furniture
and with a fine-tooth comb

searched high and low for evidence
of where she'd stashed her hoard.
She'd hid it in her Oldsmobile
and off in this she roared,

to burn along the 212,
quit Bearsville at a rate,
and didn't stop until she reached
the mighty interstate.

I 87 is its name
and here when she felt safe,
she stopped to take a look around,
this little blue-eyed waif.

A trailer, long abandoned, stood
beside a sun-scorched patch.
She tried the door and found
it had been left upon the latch.

And this is where she settled down
to make her home anew,
serving eggs with honeyed ham
and coffee freshly brewed.

If customers want porridge oats
she shows them to the door.
She loathes the fairy tale and won't
abide it any more.

She put it on the menu once
and tried it for a night.
'Too hot', 'too cold', the folks all joked.
It never was 'Just right!'

Some guys will tease her 'bout the chairs
and say that they're too small.
She let one in her bed one night
and said, 'you've got the gall

to complain of the dimensions
of my tables and my chairs,

when *that's* all you've to offer?
Now put away your wares!'

There's a diner on the interstate,
run by a blue-eyed blonde:
a girl who's known as Goldilocks,
of whom I'm rather fond.

Inspired by the chain rhyming pattern and some aspects of "Stopping by Woods on a Snowy Evening" by Robert Frost 1874-1963

The Moon Shadow

Whose horse this is I do not know;
its shadow cast upon the snow;
the moon-made shape wrought at my feet;
compels my hurrying steps to slow.

I should not linger on this street.
I have a mission to complete.
The shadow I must leave behind,
my own I dare not let it meet.

Too late! The shadows have combined!
Our destinies henceforth entwined.
The full-moon's spell I cannot fight –
to seize the mount I am resigned.

A horse-thief now in common sight
in flesh and shadow we take flight;
to ride for ever through the night;
to ride for ever through the night.

Dreaming

He's rowing me across the lake,
me dad, I think 'am I awake?'
He died in 1994,
didn't he? And what is more

he's wearing army battle dress,
though his time in service came to less
than fifteen days at Aldershot,
it says in documents I've got.

He fell while on a training course,
trying to jump a vaulting horse –
did some damage to his feet;
got sent back to civvy street.

I hope this is a dream at last.
I cleared his bank out pretty fast
the day he died in Hillingdon,
witnessed by a chilling don

from University Brunel,
who though he said he'd seen it all:
an old man clutching at his heart,
across the road declined to dart.

'cos he was late for his first lecture
of the day so his conjecture,
with two events in time conjoint,
intervening at that point

would fail the greater urgency,
at coroner's inquest he would plea.
And so the old man died alone,
with 99 on his mobile phone.

But now he's cutting 'cross the wake
of motor boats upon the lake
and looking fitter than a fish.
To have him live was once my wish,

but him alive would put me out.
My filial heart is filled with doubt.
I pinch myself – I need a sign,
for sight and memory to align.

And then without a further word,
he turns into a yellow bird.
Yet, still an inconclusive act,
for he was always doing that.

Gender Balance

Gollum the hermaphrodite
claimed loudly to possess the right
to use the "ladies'" or the "gents'".
He offered up as evidence
beneath a cloak, paraphernalia:
a complex set of genitalia.

Littleport

Littleport is a Fenland Village
five miles north of the cathedral
city of Ely. Trains from
Littleport railway station will
get you to London King's Cross
in an hour and a quarter, but
Fenlanders being what they are,
few bother. Londonders being
what they are, few come the
other way, either.
I lived in the village for a while,
singing in a local choir while I
tried to get back with a soprano
ex-girlfriend. By the time I left,
out of key and out of luck, I
found I'd managed to write a
few poems. Each contains a
trace of the real events that
inspired them.

The landlord of a riverside pub did a runner after getting into difficulties with a loan shark.

The Lone Shark

I once loved a lone shark, but the lone shark died –
mugged by some zander and a pike he'd denied
a loan for the purchase of an underwater gun.
Now the depths of the Great Ouse, by outlaws overrun,

is safe for neither eel nor fish
and river dwellers, vainly wish
the shadow of the shark were still
around to keep the peace and fill

the gap that often opens when
strong leaders fall like old Saddam,
and neighbours who did co-exist
seize upon each others tails and twist.

Revered had been the lone shark,
as he swept the waters deep.
Protection was his business,
in safety he would keep

the bream, the carp, the tench, the rudd
and very rarely was the blood

of any cold-fleshed creature spilt.
He lived on rats and otter's milk.
I suckled him myself at times
and read him children's nursery rhymes

while in return he'd chase away
all who'd with a mermaid play
their little games of grope and run,
or tweak my fish tail just for fun

No longer in Great Ouse to tarry;
back to the North Sea now to hurry.
To Copenhagen I must swim
and folk tale writers tell of him.

Down in Beck Row There Lives an Old Dame

Down in Beck Row you'll find an old dame
who lives in a field with her pigs, it's a shame
that the Council won't let her build
a home for herself and her grandson, young Will.
They've plenty of room there, acres of space.
They don't need a lot, because most of their tastes
they share with their pigs, so they won't want to wash
and rules about safety and health are all tosh – to them.

Now Will is engaged to a young sow named Sue.
They'd love to get married, but what can they do?
She lives *en famille* with the Trotters, and Dad
the old boar, though he says he'd be glad
the sow to wed off, if not now, by and by,
can't see the young couple cooped up in a sty
with the other three Trotters, Ham, Bacon and Lard,
so it seems that the wedding must wait, which is hard –
on them.

The Head of the Council, Sam Snooty by name,
declares 'I'm afraid it'd be just the same
for anyone wanting to build on this site.
I'm turning you down by the rules, not from spite.
In fact, if you're wanting advice, I'll say this:
The Council loves tourists, and if holiday bliss

you can offer to visitors here on this spot,
a caravan park could bring in a lot – of them.'

So now the old dame and her grandson, young Will,
a petition they've got going round, but until
they can prove a demand for their plan
to bring in those tourists by car or by van
they're urging their porkers to pick up their pens
and scribble out invites to all of their friends
in pig sties and cow sheds all over the Fens
to sort out their days off and come here to spend – some
of them.

The Last Panda in Littleport

The Pandas are leaving their Littleport home.
They're slipping away in the night.
The streets of the village no longer to roam
in thick fleecy coats, black and white.

Can lack of bamboo give us a clue
to the animals' dissatisfaction?
Or could jokes about police cars (they've heard not a few)
have annoyed them just more than a fraction?

If only they weren't such a pain with their food.
They won't eat a thing but bamboo.
They spit out anything else, which is rude
or groan and throw up in the loo.

We pandered too much to those creatures, I say.
We let them have all they desired,
and now they've decided to call it a day
to Chatteris, they say they've retired.

All except one, so the postman declares,
which remains in a house where the cat
has chased it around and up and down stairs.
Now it's perched on a stand with the hats.

Somebody's already rung for the vet
from the hat-stand to talk it back down.
Failing which we could borrow a butterfly net
should there be a lepidopterist around

Then we'll pat it and stroke it and tell it goodbye
as they bundle it off in a truck.
Panda's aren't easy neighbours; at least we did try.
In Chatteris they might have more luck.

Braving the Maelstrom

To sail for Bermuda, the young man planned,
a chart of the Triangle in his hand.
To Ely Marina he bid farewell
and soon of the Great Ouse he felt the swell

He'd stop at Lisbon, but not for the sights
in which he'd been told there were few delights:
the grinding dirge of fado laments;
fish that smell just like the gents

in Market Street on Friday night,
but taste far worse; at least he might
enjoy the company of eager girls,
flocking to join him across the world

to sail, and dare the maelstrom to do its worst,
as they cut and turn, the current in bursts
of energy, spelling their demise
seeks to deny him his long-sought prize:

The Flying Dutchman's ghost to see,
clad in spindrift to windward and lee.
By turning then and round about,
seizing the moment the waves to flout

and dash for freedom, escape the clutch
of the deadly current that caught the Dutch-
man, Van de Decken, in its watery grip.
And an Ely sailor's courageous trip

thenceforth will make itself the norm
for children cowering from the storm
to scare each other with in the dark
and tell of whirlpools in the River Lark.

But dreams of daring-do are fine
if sailors can avoid the lines
that anglers cast along the way.
Else glory-seekers end their day

caught up in anglers' lines and fury,
as did our young man, Malcolm Drury,
who failed to put his dreams to use
and got no further than Denver Sluice.

Lizzie's Boots

On a Fenland walking holiday
young Lizzie caught trench foot.
While camping by Vermuyden's Drain
she'd innocently put

her boots beneath an inlet pipe
and left them for the night.
When she awoke next morning,
just imagine Lizzie's plight!

Her boots were full to brimming,
though the pipe was strangely dry.
They'd been pissed in accidentally
by a local passer-by.

A summer cold had blocked her nose,
which p'rhaps is just as well.
Wet boots are bad enough themselves,
without the awful smell

that comes from leather soaked in pee,
though she was not aware
a stranger had relieved himself
in each one of the pair

She didn't have the time to give
the sun to dry them out.
From Chatteris to Ramsey takes
three hours or thereabouts.

She needed to be there by noon,
and it was half past eight.
She set off squelching noisily,
not wanting to be late.

In 'The Jolly Sailor' public bar,
she met up with the troupe.
She thought the members nice enough
but none was cock-a-hoop.

For the odour from poor Lizzie's boots
did nothing to improve
the earthy smell of Fenland folk.
A vote to make a move

was unanimously carried –
no need for show of hands.
Outside, the walkers formed themselves
into impromptu bands.

The numbers varied, some had five
and others four or three

but none included Lizzie.
It was pitiful to see

how when she tried to join a group
they'd quickly split apart,
reforming once she'd wandered off.
She tried not to lose heart.

At first she struggled to maintain
the leader's rapid pace,
but when he broke into a run,
an ever growing space

grew up between the sorry girl
and those who from her sped.
Even weakling stragglers found
the strength to keep ahead

until at last she realised
they'd disappeared from sight.
She had no compass or a map,
so when at last the night

closed in, she didn't have a clue
which drain was which, what field.
For Fenland mud looks much the same
whatever crop it yields.

She pitched her tent against a barn
but didn't have the strength
to take her clothes off, nor her boots
she stretched her body's length

on lumpy ground, a 'Crunchy Bar'
was all she had to eat.
Yet sleep soon came despite the throb
of aching, sodden feet.

Of what she dreamed, we cannot know,
for she did not recall,
when she was woken suddenly
by the loud insistent bawl

of a cow requiring milking
and the shouting of a man;
the grating of a rusty hinge;
the clattering of a pan.

She stretched and yawned and wondered
what more she could endure,
though p'rhaps her luck had changed
– a strange conclusion to be sure,

seeing she was trespassing
on God-Knows-Who's terrain

but she was keen for company
whatever it entrained.

She poked her head out from the tent –
the day was barely dawning.
She gave both cow and man a smile
and wished them each "Good morning!"

The man and cow exchanged a look,
though let us cast no slurs.
If they shared one brain between them,
the larger half was hers.

Blank of face and toothless,
there was earth upon his feet.
He had six fingers on each hand,
the IQ of the peat

on which he stood was fifteen points
above this dullard's own,
and yet he had a heart of gold,
for this and this alone

he towered over other men
in soul and moral stature.
Name any great philanthropist,
they're likely not a patch–er

– pon this selfless Fenland saint
who tended Lizzie's feet,
while she sat on a milking stool.
The milk was warm and sweet.

She drank it from the milking pail
while he dried out her boots
and rubbed her feet with whale oil
which nobody disputes

is the perfect way to treat trench foot,
though where he got the stuff
is really anybody's guess.
To her it was enough

to have her small appendages
relieved of cold and pain.
They very soon began to feel
quite normal once again.

"You've been so kind," she told the man,
"but now I'd better go."
He offered to direct her
if she would let him know

where she was headed, but of course
she didn't have a clue.

She'd have to find out where she was
before she could review

the progress of her holiday,
walking in the Fens.
There's water here enough, she mused
to get the divers' bends.

When she asked him where they were right now
he sprayed through toothless gums,
"You're a sparrow's spit from Chatteris."
She dared not do the sums

to calculate the miles she'd trudged
to end up where she'd started.
He walked her to the Ramsey road.
They hugged before they parted.

A few yards on she turned her head
to look at him again.
He was pissing by an inlet pipe
into Vermuyden's Drain.

Acknowledgements

My thanks go to: Liz Cashden, poet and creative writing tutor for WEA in Sheffield, for providing the inspiration that was to turn me into a poet; Roy Blackman – The Yorkshire Memory Man – singer-songwriter, for getting me up on stage for the first time at the 'Nelly Dean' in Rotherham; Tim Wilson, author and creative writing tutor at City College, Peterborough for his continuing inspiration and example; Dr Rosemary Westwell, writer and broadcaster for nagging me into publishing this collection.

Made in the USA
Charleston, SC
24 March 2014